Gabriele Ebert

Maurice Frydman

The active life of a close disciple

of Ramana Maharshi and Nisargadatta Maharaj

© 2025 Gabriele Ebert

Verlag: BoD · Books on Demand GmbH, In de Tarpen 42,
22848 Norderstedt, bod@bod.de
Druck: Libri Plureos GmbH, Friedensallee 273, 22763 Hamburg
ISBN: 978-3-7693-3899-7

Inhalt

Introduction

Not much is known about the Pole Maurice Frydman (1894 or 1901–1976), although he was an important figure in the circle of Mahatma Gandhi, the Aundh experiment of the Indian princely state of Aundh, Ramana Maharshi, Nisargadatta Maharaj and Jiddu Krishnamurti. He promoted the exchange of literature between India and Poland, helped Tibetan refugees to find a place to stay in India after the Chinese invasion of Tibet, and was involved in planning the Dalai Lama's flight to India. He also compiled "Maharshi's Gospel", a collection of questions and answers with the Maharshi, which contains many of his own questions, and translated Nisargadatta Maharaj's conversations with visitors from Marathi tape recordings into English, resulting in the extensive work "I Am That".

Maurice was a karma yogi who took immediate action. He left nothing biographical behind and always kept himself in the background. The sources are therefore sparse.

Apa Pant, the son of the raja of the princely state of Aundh, reports the most about him. V. Ganesan, the great-nephew of Ramana Maharshi, has dedicated a chapter to him in his book "Ramana Perya Puranam", David Godman spoke freely about him in an interview, and Srinivasan has tried to compile the facts in an online document. There is also an account of Barry Gordon's experiences in Maurice's later years.

Maurice's life is unique among the disciples of Ramana Maharshi and Nisargadatta Maharaj in its emphasis on action and is also of interest in relation to the history of India. It is therefore certainly worth a read.

Maurice Frydman's life:

Apa Pant reports

Maurice Frydman

Apa Pant (1912-1992) was the eldest son of Bhawanrao Shriniwasrao Pant Pratinidhi, the Raja of Aundh, one of the many princely states in British India. In 1937, after his studies in England, he met Maurice Frydman for the first time and remained associated with him until his death. He regarded him not only as a friend but also as his guru and wrote a detailed article for the Ramanashram magazine "The Mountain Path", which is reproduced here in full:[1]

---

[1] With kind permission of Ramanashram, Tiruvannamalai, India. The text has been supplemented with own comments.

"I must indeed have earned a great deal of punya (spiritual merit) in many a past life to have deserved to meet with such a unique guide, friend and philosopher as Swami Bharatananda, alias Maurice Frydman. Although he ever kept his personality in the background, his influence on events and individuals, always operating simultaneously at different levels of consciousness, has been incalculable.

It has been Maurice who was the active instrument for me to meet four of the greatest sages of our times. He propelled me to Sri Ramana Maharshi within a few months of my arrival from England in 1937 after the completion of my studies. With Sri J. Krishnamurti, an encounter that was to last over fifty years started at the instigation of Maurice. It was also Maurice who introduced me to Mahatma Gandhi and I thenceforth became a regular visitor at Sevagram[1]. And finally in 1975, only a few weeks before he left the body, his last act was that of taking me to Sri Nisargadatta Maharaj.

His life of experimentation and of experience was linked up with the message and work of these four great souls. But Maurice made us all – his friends and devotees – fellow-pilgrims on his path, urging, advising, often brow-beating us to be sincere, simple, truthful. He would steadily gaze at you, look into you, through you, with those kindly, piercing eyes silently, compassionately, and uncover instantly all your quirks and problems, physical, emotional, mental, spiritual. He would then relentlessly take you to task for your lapses and immediately offer correct, direct, but often undigestible and even disturbing advice. Revolutionary changes have been brought into many lives after a moment's contact with Maurice Frydman.

---

[1] Gandhi lived in the village of Sevagram near Wardha in Maharashtra from 1936 until his assassination in 1948.

That is exactly what happened to me that November in 1937 when I was unexpectedly confronted with Maurice Frydman in Bangalore.

Bhawanrao Shriniwasrao Pant Pratinidhi, Raja of Aundh State, 1922

I had just returned from a four-and-a-half-year study period at Oxford and London, a very bright-eyed young lad who imagined himself to be a 'revolutionary communist'. I wanted to fight the British Raj and establish communism in India – in fact, a new Utopia! I was my fathers, – Raj Bhawanrao's eldest surviving son. He was 61 years old then, and I was 25. He understood my enthusiasm and also my impulsiveness. He arranged for me to get a 3-month 'training' in administration in Mysore State, then the most ideal and well-run of the 675 princely states of India. Father also gave me a private secretary to look after me, a chauffeur together with a new car, and a servant. Within one week of my arrival in Bangalore I was in full form and thoroughly enjoying myself with this period of 'princely' training.

A strict timetable of 'visits to institutions and factories', followed by 'briefings and discussions' was arranged. One such visit was to the Government Electrical Factory on the outskirts of Bangalore. Sri Bharatananda – Maurice Frydman – had been its Director and Chief Executive since 1935.

Being 'foreign returned' and a Prince, I was habituated to being treated very deferentially. I, on my side, always wore my best Oxford accent and a condescending princely smile with assumed courtesy. Maurice, on the other hand, was in a very bad mood. A year before, he had taken sannyas and had begun to live according to his vows. When it was reported to Sir Mirza Ismail that his brilliant and efficient Engineer-Director had shaved his head and taken sannyasa that he went to work in saffron robes, begged for his daily bread, and gave away all his wages (Rs. 3,000 per month) to the poor and needy, the Grand Vizier was furious. He sent for 'that Mr. Frydman' to remind him that he had hired an engineer, not a sannyasi and forbade him henceforth to wear gerua.

Maurice, on his side, preferred his resignation on the spot, saying that how and what he ate or wore was his personal matter, and that he must be free to follow his own pattern of life so long as 'I satisfy all those concerned with the quality of my work as an engineer and manager.' A compromise was finally reached according to which Maurice would have to wear European or Mysore dress only when a VIP visited the factory. As he had to put on a suit for my sake, Maurice was in his darkest mood!

As I got out of the car, Maurice was waiting at the doorstep, but instead of returning my smile, he gruffly said, 'Well, young

Prince, do you know anything of electricity or will I be wasting my time on you?'

I, of course, quickly stepped back into the car and started to slam the door shut, when Maurice realized his mistake and almost dragged me out of the car. 'I did not mean to offend you. Forgive me', he apologised, and I saw for the first time that winning smile spread over his suntanned face. Within five minutes of all this drama our vibrations had clicked. And they remained clicked for forty years, until his death on 9th March 1976, and further, till this present time.

From the word go, I was deeply impressed by Maurice's systematic, well-ordered, highly disciplined personality. His intelligence was overpowering; his simplicity scintillating; his spontaneous, genuine love overwhelming. There was nothing false, superficial or superfluous about Maurice. His response to his environment was always razor-sharp and instantaneous, always compassionate. There was never a gap between what he saw and felt and his immediate action. If he saw a beggar in rags he gave him all his food and his shirt as well without ever theorising about it. There were no dogmas, no theories, no hypotheses; only spontaneous, direct action. He belonged to no political party, religion or 'ism'.

Once, in Bombay in 1943, my wife Nalini, who was then practising surgery (gynaecology) in the villages of my father's state, Aundh, was talking with him of her work-plan. She spoke of the financial difficulties of poor Aundh in acquiring even the necessary rudimentary equipment. Maurice asked, 'How much money do you require immediately?' Nalini said offhand, 'Ten thousand rupees', which was then a large sum. Next morning in walks Maurice with Rs.10,000/- in Rs. 100 notes! 'Nalini, start work!' he said. That was the way my guru taught: direct, compassionate action, by practical example.

Maurice Frydman was born in 1894[1] in the Jewish ghetto of Krakaw in Southern Poland, then a part of tsarist Russia.

From the accounts that Maurice gave out grudgingly from time to time during our long and close association, it seems that his family was very poor. His father, a devout Jew, worked in the synagogue. His mother sewed, washed clothes and cooked, and brought up her children as best she could, though there was hardly any money to do so. Maurice did not taste white bread until he was thirteen. He acquired his first toothbrush when he was fifteen!

But Maurice was a born genius. He was reading and writing in the Cyrillic, Roman and Hebrew alphabets and speaking fluent Russian, Polish, French, English and Hebrew before he was

---

[1] According to another source, he was born on 20.10.1901 in the capital Warsaw in a house with the number 5541, father: Icek Lejba Frydman, mother: Mariem. His Polish name was Maurycy Frydman or Maurycy Frydman-Mor, in the anglicized version Maurice Frydman. cf. https://www.wikitree.com/wiki/Frydman-16#_note-0

ten. His father wanted Maurice, his eldest son, to become a rabbi and lead a secure, holy and useful life of service to the 'chosen people', who were suffering under the heel of tsarist authority and thus help them survive the persecution generated by the prevalent racial intolerance.

However, Maurice's capabilities were early recognized by his teachers, who thus enabled him to accomplish the all-too-rare feat of a Jew entering the tsarist Russian school in his area.

He proved himself exceptionally brilliant and, having stood first amongst 500 boys in his high school final examinations, he sat for the Central Scholarship Examination and got 95%, standing first in the province of Poland. For this he received a State scholarship, and opted for what was then his strongest urge, a course in electrical engineering. Before he was 20 he had about 100 patents to his name for his electrical and mechanical inventions, of which a 'talking book' was one.

Soon he was picked up by the laboratories and then research institutes, and by 1925 had travelled over much of Europe and worked in German, Dutch and Danish industrial establishments.

By the age of 25, however, what was to be his life-long urge had come desperately to the surface. He wanted to 'see God'. For a few years he had seriously studied the Talmud and other Jewish religious books. Judaism, however, did not satisfy for long the incisive, logical, courageous, non-dogmatic mind of Maurice.

Maurice then converted to Russian Orthodoxy and became a monk, retreating to a solitary monastery in the Carpathian mountains in southern Poland. One incident during this period clearly illustrates Maurice's character. It seems that one day 'Satan' tempted him to jump over a mighty waterfall to 'prove his faith' in Jesus Christ and the Church. So this intrepid seeker after truth immediately jumped down a 100-foot precipice! He was saved by a few shrubs in which his cassock (robes) got entangled. This was typical Maurice! This is what inspired and was loved by thousands during his 78-year span of life on this earth.

Annie Besant and Krishnamurti, 1927

By 1926 Maurice had got 'sick and tired', as he once told us, of all orthodox dogmas: 'Believe this, don't do this, do this, follow me – didn't suit me,' he said. He wanted to seek freely everywhere and try desperately to find out for himself 'what all this is about'. It was at about this time that he came in touch with the Theosophical Society and met Annie Besant and J. Krishnamurti. In the Swiss Alps and many times at Saanen in

Holland, he met Krishnaji[1]. For nearly fifty years Maurice was 'very, very close to Krishnaji', and the most serious and obstinate questioner of this great seer.

By 1928 he was ready to emigrate to France in search of a job and 'new adventures', as he put it. He arrived in Paris with high hopes, no money and nowhere to stay. But soon he saw an advertisement in Paris Soire about a new electrical factory that was being started in the outskirts of the city. He applied and was immediately accepted. By 1934 he had become the General Manager of the factory.

All this while, his real urge to 'find and meet God' was not forgotten. He read voraciously books on religion, mysticism and occultism. He continuously experimented on himself with whatever practice he was reading about in the vast section on these subjects in the Biblioteque Nationale in Paris.

Then suddenly he hit upon Vedanta. In translation (French and German) he poured over the Upanishads, the Gita, the Mahabharata. Paul Brunton's books on Ramana Maharshi attracted him greatly. This was his first introduction to this great master and what was, for Maurice, the greatest revelation: 'Who am I?'.

During this period, Maurice's one and incessant wish was to reach India somehow. Any wish, when it becomes desperately urgent, is fulfilled, and this was what happened to Maurice.

In 1935 Sir Mirza Ismail[2], the extraordinary and visionary Diwan of Mysore, was on a tour of England and Europe, seeking to recruit able engineering and managerial talent for the projected Government Electrical Factory in Bangalore. The Government had suggested that he visit some important factories in

---

[1] Krishnamurti was reverentially called Krishnaji.
[2] Mirza Ismail was Diwan (Prime Minister) of the princely states of Mysore, Jaipur and Hyderabad. According to other sources, he travelled to Europe as early as 1934.

France to facilitate his search. This search led him to the very factory of which Maurice was the Managing Director.

Mirza Ismail, Diwan of Mysore (1883-1959), ca. 1930

How deeply impressed was this remarkable administrator and statesman, Sir Mirza Ismail, by the personality and work of Maurice Frydman can be gauged by the remark he casually made during his two-hour visit. 'Mr. Frydman, I wish you were free to come and at least visit us in Mysore and advise us about development.' Sir Mirza had in mind a replica of this very Paris factory in far-off Bangalore.

Maurice's reply was again typical of him: 'Sir, my bags are packed. I am ready to leave with you!'

Thus Maurice came to India, his dream country, and fulfilled not only his own destiny but helped many like me to fulfil theirs, too.

MAURICE FREDMAN

Within two years of his arrival Maurice had the Government Electrical Factory in Bangalore producing transformers, switch-gears, resistors, insulators – all that was urgently required to satisfy the growing need for electrical energy in this modern, progressive state.

Within six months of his arrival in India, Maurice had become an ardent disciple of Sri Ramana Maharshi, the sage of Arunachala.[1] He worked in Bangalore all week and then hurried to Tiruvannamalai to spend his weekends with the Maharshi. Maurice had begged Sri Bhagavan to grant him sannyas. He said he wanted to renounce the world and seek enlightenment.

---

[1] more about Ramana Maharshi s. Chapter further back

Sri Bhagavan characteristically refused him sannyas saying, 'I have no ochre clothes for you, Sir, and you do not need them!'

Swami Ramdas (1884-1963)

But Maurice was nothing if he was not pugnaciously adamant and self-willed. He went to Swami Ramdas at Anandashram in Kanhangad and took his vows from him. A Hindu name, Swami Bharatananda, was given to him. He shaved his head, threw away his European clothes, dressed in the saffron robes of a mendicant, and vowed to beg for his food – for which purposes he went to the extent of procuring a traditional begging bowl. This was also typical of Maurice. There was never with him anything 'put on' or for show, hypocritical, false or sham. He was always 1,00,000% genuine and it was this earnest adherence to conviction followed by immediate, spontaneous action that spurred him on to fulfil this desire for renunciation when once it had emerged in his soul. But the outward garb and rigid ideas about the meaning of sannyas gradually fell away from him due to his continued contact with Ramana Maharshi and J. Krishnamurti.

By 1947 he was free of these externalities. But this was not before he had his confrontation with Sir Mirza which resulted in our rather stormy first meeting.

From the very first day we met, after the initial conflict, Maurice, as it were, 'took me in hand'. Without my knowing it, he started to guide me to the correct path for me. He was far, far ahead of me but would lovingly, patiently wait for me to catch up with him. He was never angry or irritated by my innumerable 'princely' (and other) stupidities.

I do not know when we truly became 'fellow pilgrims'. But on that pleasantly cool December morning in 1937 when we reached Ramanashram I felt that something very, very strange and significant was happening to me and that without him to lead me, 'IT' could not be happening to me at all. I think we stayed at the Ashram for a few days.

Maurice made me do my daily suryanamaskars[1] in front of the Maharshi. Sri Bhagavan only smiled and said, 'After a couple of hours of meditation this sadhana is good for you to loosen up your limbs'. I have never forgotten it, and even at this age (79) I remember those words when I wake up to samsara each dawn and do my suryanamaskars.

At Ramanashram there was simply 'NOTHING' – no talk, no listening, no questions, no hoping, no fear, no prayer, no movement of the mind or the intellect at all. But my turbulent, arrogant ego had nothing to grasp on to. In a way it was bewildered but watchful of itself. But it was certainly lost. I could not 'figure' it at all.

---

[1] the sun salutation, a special way of bowing, a yoga exercise

Ramana Maharshi (1879-1950)

The first night Maurice and I were in a small hut sleeping on mattresses on the floor. The whole night I heard voices arguing loudly, trumpets blaring, and the beating of big and small drums. I was certain that I did not get a wink of sleep all night. When I, not a little irritated, shouted at Maurice about all this 'hullaballoo' during the night, he said, 'Apa, there was no noise. All was "joyfully peaceful". Your tortured mind alone made all the noise. Watch it.'

I learned later that the mind may be extremely subtle. It may work faster than the speed of light, yet often it takes longer than your body to make a journey, so that you arrive, as it were, in two instalments. Maurice often refused to speak with me for a full twenty-four hours, saying, 'Apa, your body only has arrived. I will wait till you arrive before I communicate with you.'

Almost immediately afterwards, Maurice took me to J. Krishnamurti. Krishnaji was spending a few days in Poona that winter, and Rausahib Patwardhan, Achyut Patwardhan, Maurice and I spent as much time as he would allow us with him during those glorious ten days.

I marvelled at the incisive brilliance and insight of Maurice as he challenged and argued almost every point with Krishnaji. It was not the challenge of the arrogant or self-assured pandit. Rather, Maurice responded to what Krishnaji was explaining through his own immediate experience of what he was saying. He was experiencing it at that very moment. In this 'duel' between the two of them, there was no memory of the past or any conjecture about the future. It was all happening Now and Here, from moment to moment. It was ever fresh, new and fragrant.

During my fateful visit to Bangalore in 1937, Maurice and I had planned one innovation after another for my father's small, impoverished state of Aundh. The atmosphere hummed with new ideas and plans for the development of village communities and the introduction of science and technology into them, which was a particularly keen issue with Maurice.

'Science and technology must be taken to the villages and made simple for the use of the peasants,' he declared. Thus inspired, I had gone to pay my farewell call on Sir Mirza Ismail. I wanted him to 'loan' Maurice to me for six months so that we two together could chalk out a plan for the development of the 75 villages of Aundh. When I had made my appeal, Sir Mirza looked glum and said, 'Let your father, the Rajasaheb, write to me, and we will see what we can do for you.'

When the letter from Aundh went out to Bangalore with my father's signature, back came the answer: 'We cannot spare the services of Mr. Maurice Frydman at the moment.' In diplomatic language 'at the moment' always means 'never' and also 'do not write again'. Period!

Sir Mirza should have realised that his refusal to lend Maurice to Aundh for a short while would have the opposite effect. And so it happened that as I sat brooding one morning in the Rama Hall of my father's palace, in walks Maurice Frydman with a bundle of gerua clothes at the end of a stick!

'I have come, Apa,' he said simply. 'Sir Mirza cannot dictate to me. I am nobody's slave. I have left Mysore and come to stay with you permanently. Let us work!'[1]

'Good God!' I exclaimed. 'But ...', I spluttered, 'Aundh State cannot afford to pay you Rs. 3,000 per month and give you a free house and a car and an office! Why, the highest paid official in the State, the Diwan, gets Rs. 75, with the Muslim chauffeur, Haji Master, next at Rs. 70!'

Maurice laughed his rumbling, guttural laugh. 'I shall sleep in that corner on the floor, opposite you. Give me an Indian desk of the old style to write on. Your mother will feed me. I have my legs to walk on. You can also walk with me. That is all. We will work together for Aundh. Now give me food!'

That was typical Maurice. Telegraphic, often Morse-code-style staccato speech which carried the necessary meaning without a superfluous word.

It was the pen of Maurice that wrote down the inspired ideas of Mahatma Gandhi, bringing decentralised democracy to the villages of the state of Aundh, which was then ruled by my father.[2]

---

[1] Maurice Frydman was in charge of the princely state of Aundh from 1938.

[2] David Godman tells us that Maurice had already seen Gandhi in Paris.

This 'rash' act upset not only the British, but also the other princely states, whose rulers never thought of any authority other than themselves as supreme in their states. Thus we soon found ourselves in that famous mud hut talking with the Mahatma.

The Mahatma briefly greeted Swami Bharatananda with, 'So you have caught hold of the poor Raja of Aundh now, and left the rich one in Mysore to his destiny?' The Mahatma then went directly to the point and suggested that in fact the ruler should be 'the first servant of the people and the keeper of their conscience'. The drama of all these happenings I have related in two of my books, 'A Moment In Time' and 'An Unusual Raja', both published by Orient Longman. [1]

"He [Frydman] was running his electrical factory in Paris. He was walking down the street and he saw a bit of a crowd at one of the train stations and wandered over to see what it was. And there was Mahatma Gandhi on the platform in Paris, of all places, changing trains. In those days if you wanted to go from London – he had just been to a conference in London – back to India, the quickest way was to get a train across Europe and then get a boat in Greece. But for that he had to change trains in Paris, and Maurice just happened to be on the platform for the two minutes that Gandhi spent in Paris to watch him change trains. He said, 'I looked at this man. I fell in love with him immediately. I fell in love with the idea of India and I just knew I had to go.'"
https://www.wisdom2be.com/essays-insights-wisdomwritings-spirituality/david-godman-interview-buddha-and-the-gas-pump-excerpt-on-maurice-frydman
[1] Godman describes Apa Pant and Maurice's visit to Gandhi as follows:
"Gandhi said, 'It is a very nice idea but you can't cut people loose like this. If you want my endorsement of this project, you both have to agree to live there for a number of years. You have to teach these people how to be independent, how to look after themselves.' And then he jabbed his finger at the raja's son. He said, 'You can't live in a palace. You are going there to try and convince these village people that village life is a good, viable way of living. They are not going to respect you if you rock up every day in a big car from the palace.

Mahatma Gandhi, 1931

After returning from the epoch-making visit to the Mahatma, Maurice literally buried himself in the wilderness of Aundh. He went about on foot visiting each of the 75 villages of the state[1] and then set up his headquarters under a thorny acacia tree, with little shade to protect him from the elements. This acacia was located in a dry, waterless plateau of what is now western Maharashtra, 75 miles east of the capital of Aundh. And it was here that he remained for three years.

Build yourself a mud hut in one of these villages, live there for ten years and demonstrate to your people that this kind of life can be a rewarding, productive way of life.' And so Maurice and Apa Pant, as he was called, looked at each other and said ok. Gandhi signed." Ibid.
[1] Maurice went from village to village and taught the people carpentry, plumbing, technology and everything else they needed to know.

The daily temperature used to be around 120° F, and at night the mercury would drop suddenly to around 20° F, with a bitter, dry wind. There was no hut or any other shelter for Maurice, so he used to wrap himself up in bamboo matting covered with the coarsely woven blankets spun from the local wool. It was very hard Tapasya [renunciation], indeed!

While he was still in the capital of Aundh, Maurice had made the Raja abolish capital punishment by a special decree. Now, feeling with full empathy the sorrow and shame of the shackled convicts in the Atpadi jail, he rushed to the capital to beg the Raja for the 'loan' of 25 of the 'most desperate' and dangerous of these convicts for his colony. Bhawanrao, as usual, responded spontaneously to this objective compassion (karuna) of Swami Bharatananda and, with Haji Abdul Aziz, Maurice established in 1939 the first ever 'Free Prison', not only in Aundh, but in the whole of India. [1]

These 'dangerous desperados' were allowed to bring their families to Swatantrapur (City of the Free), where they could, on parole, visit their own villages as well. It was a revolution in itself. It brought a new dimension to the whole range of relationships between man and man, man and authority, and man and nature.

These 'free' citizens dug a huge well which, in that arid desert area, was a miracle in itself. It struck a pocket of extremely sweet water in the sandy loam soil, and plenty of it. Hundreds from Atpadi and other villages visited this well and sat with wonderment and devotion in their eyes at the feet of this cherubic foreigner in sannyasi clothes with the enchanting smile and the perpetual glint of mischief in his eyes. The poor

---

[1] Godman: „He went off and built a village [Swatantrapur] with the aid of these prisoners. He taught them how to build houses, he taught them agriculture; he taught them all the skills they needed to live independent lives and the recidivism rate was [zero. Not a single one of these people ever needed to go back to jail." Ibid.

peasants of Aundh always felt purified in the presence of 'the Swami', whose karuna left an indelible mark on the villagers of Aundh. Swatantrapur still exists and tries to survive.[1]

Haji Abdul 'Master', now 91, visits it from time to time, and his eyes fill with tears when he thinks and feels the presence of Maurice there.

It was also around this time that Maurice became inspired with the idea of an Indo-Polish library. Uma Devi, a genteel and celebrated Polish aristocrat, had come to India a few years before Maurice and was already well set in the Ramana Maharshi – Krishnamurti – Mahatma Gandhi circuit. I do not know whether they ever met each other in Poland, but they teamed up in India to produce about 50 books through this Indo-Polish library. All of them were translations of original Sanskrit texts. How this 'treasonable' literature was smuggled, chiefly through Polish prisoners of war in India, is a thrilling story in itself. Thousands of copies of these books entered Poland, and now the demand for such books there is growing apace.[2]

---

[1] This project was so famous that the Bollywood film "Do Aankhen Barah Haath" (Two Eyes, Twelve Hands) was made about it in 1957. Maurice was hired as a technical consultant. He went to the location and made sure that everything was recorded correctly. The director wanted to name him in the movie in this capacity, but Maurice wouldn't let him.

[2] Uma Devi, born Wanda Dynowska in St. Petersburg and of aristocratic Polish descent, was a writer, translator and social activist who had come to India a few years before Frydman. Together they founded the Polish-Indian Library in Madras in 1944 and translated around fifty sacred texts into Polish (including the Bhagavad Gita, Mahabharata and Ramayana) as well as contemporary Indian poetry and literature from Sanskrit and other Indian languages. They also translated the great Polish poets into English and Indian languages. The books had to be smuggled into the country because of the Communist government in Poland after the Second World War.

During this time, Frydman and Uma Devi were also successful in bringing a large number of Polish orphans, who had been displaced

Ramana Maharshi, Maurice and Uma Devi

The sufferings and sad plight of the Tibetans in 1958-59 – the total overwhelming of an ancient, compassionate culture – was devastatingly disturbing to Maurice. He was staying with us in Sikkim at that time, watching the Tibetans fleeing in terror by the thousands and being helplessly lost in India. They were seeking shelter in the land of the birth of Gautama the Buddha, but they had no shelter, not to mention comfort. The government of Jawaharlal Nehru did not know what, where or how to do 'something' for them. It was dangerous to try to settle them near the Indo-Tibetan frontiers. Spies and agent provocateurs were everywhere, preparing for the 1962 'war of liberation' on India.

Maurice saw all this not through the eyes of a diplomat or a politician who plays for power, but as a simple, compassionate human being. For him, to feel was to act. One day he sat down

---

by the Soviet annexation of eastern Poland in 1939 and subsequently interned in Siberia, from Siberia via Iran to India before they were returned to Poland.

and drafted a letter portraying his anguish, as from me to Prime Minister Nehru, which he carried himself to Delhi. He then sat in the Prime Minister's office until the latter agreed to write letters to various state governments to grant land for the use of the Tibetan refugees. Armed with these letters Maurice, at his own expense, travelled to various states where state land above 3,500 feet was available. For two long hard years he ceaselessly laboured, touring the whole of India seeking suitable sites where the poor, neglected Tibetans could be settled. He cajoled, shouted, brow-beat bureaucrats, politicians, priests, peasants – but got land and money to create five settlements where thousands of uprooted Tibetans were rehabilitated. Were it not for Maurice this would never have happened! History will certainly record a deep sense of gratitude to Maurice Frydman – Polish Jew and Indian mystic-saint – for the inestimable and timely help that he brought for the preservation of Tibet's distinct, precious culture and identity.

Ekagrata, single-pointedness, can achieve anything, he used to say to us, who were always grateful to him. 'Yogah Karmasu Kaushalam' [Yoga is skill in action], he used to say.

Whether with Bhagavan, the Mahatma or J. Krishanamurti, Maurice's method of questioning everything, experimenting and experiencing for himself the truth at each level, and then alone accepting it, was always infallible. Even the Mahatma's experiments with food paled before those Maurice tried on himself. He always had a queer range of eatables and drinkables on the table when one sat to eat with him. One never knew what to expect nor dared one ask what they were made of. In Atpadi, together with another food experimenter, Dr. Appa Bhagwat, he extended his experiment to include a variety of grasses, roots, leaves, flowers, tree barks, and even earth. How he survived these experiments on himself is nothing short of a miracle.

Apa Pant with Indira Gandhi and the Queen of Bhutan

Once, whilst staying with us in Sikkim, he and his constant companion and fellow-pilgrim, Hilla Petit, a gracious Parsi lady, and her adopted daughter, Babulal, were crossing a windy pass in the high Himalayas. But Maurice had to be carried in a litter because, having undertaken some new experiment in dieting, he was incapable of staying on his horse. At the pass some 16,700 feet high, the bearers of the litter decided that Maurice had died and left him in the cold snowy rubble of the glacier and ran away!

Tibetans are generally afraid of corpses. Only a rescue team from ten miles away bringing flasks of hot coffee and warm blankets saved Maurice from actually fulfilling the Tibetans' fears. Experiment and experience – even unto death – this was his credo. He knew no fear. For Death he had only LOVE –

which, as he proclaimed through his objective compassionate ACTION, conquers all – even death.[1]

'The sage is dying', whispered a soft, sad voice over the trunk phone from Bombay. 'He is asking for you. Come as soon as you can.'

So my wife and I rushed, with Avalokita our youngest, his favourite, whom he had blessed in Sikkim when she was only a few months old.

When we arrived Hilla, the doctors and nurse all complained to me that Maurice was refusing to eat or take medicine. Hilla and Babulal were in tears. They implored me to 'make' Maurice eat and take his medicine, as if anyone could ever make him do anything that he didn't want to do!

There he lay in his familiar room, with everything meticulously clean and in its proper place. As I approached him, he shouted at me, 'Apa, who is dying?'

The next day he drove everyone out of the room, ordering them to leave him alone with me. Then he said, 'Apa, I hear the music, I see the bright light. Who dies? No one is dying. This diseased body is keeping me away from that Harmony and Beauty. Do not let them keep me in this body. Go now in peace.'

The next day we were all at his bedside as he breathed his last three breaths – 'Hari Om!' Sri Nisargadatta Maharaj was also by his side. I asked him, 'Maharaj, where is Maurice going? What is happening to him?'

He replied, 'Nothing is happening. No one is dying, for no one was born.'

'Then why this sense of sorrow, emptiness, loss?' I asked.

---

[1] Apa Pant makes a leap in time here. For more details on the last years of Frydman's life, see the following chapter.

'Who is feeling sorrow, emptiness, loss?' he asked.

And within hours, in the presence of Sri Nisargadatta Maharaj, the remains of what we called Maurice Frydman were consumed in the electric fire. The elements returned to their original order.

In one of his talks, Sri Nisargadatta Maharaj has said that attachment to name and form (nama-rupa) creates fear in man's heart. One who knows that he has no name or form, who is Nothing, will be afraid of nothing, including death. Maurice had reached the state of shunyata (nothingness, emptiness), he lived shunyata, and the egos he touched were thrown into a bottomless well, while their souls caught a glimpse of this ineffable state. Nevertheless, in a way quite tangible to me, Maurice is not gone. He is, as always, here, and now, a constant inspiration to love, to serve, to be fearless, sincere, and full of joy![1]

---

[1] Apa Pant: Maurice Frydman, in: The Mountain Path, Aradhana Issue 1991, pp. 31-36 and Jayanti Issue 1991, pp. 125-128

The later Years

David Godman reports that Maurice had already come across Krishnamurti as a teenager in Warsaw and spent all his pocket money for a week on a second-hand French copy of a Krishnamurti book.

Maurice with Krishnamurti

Maurice had met Krishnamurti in Switzerland and Holland in 1926, when he was still being treated as a world teacher in the Theosophical Society, but was already slowly beginning to break away from it. In 1930 he broke with the Theosophic Society and became an independent lecturer who travelled the world until his death in 1986, proclaiming: "Truth is a pathless land." One had to free oneself from all religions, institutions and external as well as internal authorities. Maurice met him often and discussed things with him. He organized meetings for him in Paris and translated some of his writings into French.

He wrote about Krishnamurti:

"From time to time the multipersonal entity that is mankind produces a man of wisdom and compassion. He knows the hearts of beings and Truth beyond the fleeting. In himself he bridges the gap between the apparent and the real and calls everyone to use him for crossing the chasm of beginningless illusion.

Krishnamurti is one of such. The Truth he wants to take us to is as ancient [as] the heart of being, but the way he shows is supremely adapted to the present state of human mind.

We have lost all confidence in whatever the past has created. Our religions, cultures and civilizations have betrayed us. We are at the brink of the abyss between nuclear warfare and overpopulation. And we do not know whom to trust, whom to follow.

Krishnamurti says: trust nobody, follow nobody. Doubt – question – see the false of false and the so-called true too as false. Distrust even your own capacity for doubt, till your mind realizes fully that not only it is unable to reach the truth, but it creates illusion ceaselessly. The understanding of the perverting nature of the mind is all the mind can reach. Total self-distrust leads to a state of infinite despair. The mind has nothing to turn to and yet cannot stand the agony of nothingness. Having nowhere to go it does what it never did before – it goes within – along a new dimension – and meets at last the power of the loving wisdom of the Fact.

Krishnamurti has an enormous reverence for facts. To him the fact contains all that is needed to deal with it creatively and happily. All that we need is a mind able to meet a fact in humility and obedience. We do it in science and in love and in pure action born from reverence for truth and life."[1]

Apa Pant has written little about Maurice's later years. After Mahatma Gandhi was assassinated in 1948 and Ramana Maharshi died in 1950, he went to Bangalore and helped establish the Rishi Valley School – one of Krishnamurti's schools. He managed and coordinated the extensive activities of the Krishnamurti Foundation at the Rajghat Center in Varanasi (Benaras) and often fought intellectual duels with Krishnamurti over his philosophy and Vedanta.

A major new field of activity opened up for Maurice when the Chinese invaded Tibet and thousands of Tibetans fled across the Himalayas to India, where they found little protection. They had neither food nor shelter. India was on familiar terms with China, did not want to anger the Chinese and therefore remained inactive. Jawaharlal Nehru said bluntly: "My hands are tied." Who should step up to the plate to solve the refugee problem? Only Apa Pant remained, who fortunately was the governor of Sikkim at that time. He invited his long-time friend Maurice to stay in Sikkim for a few months as his guest.

Maurice said to him: "You are going to be of great use to me! We have an important mission to accomplish here because we have to save His Holiness the Dalai Lama, all the old Buddhist manuscripts and thousands of Tibetans."[2]

Both Maurice and Achyut Patwardhan had worked out a plan for the Dalai Lama's escape and how to get the Tibetan scriptures out of the country. Maurice got Nehru to sign an agreement that the Dalai Lama could come to India in 1959 on the condition that he did not come as a political leader. He was allowed to be the spiritual leader of the Tibetans in exile, could

---

[1] Maurice Frydman: How I understand Krishnamurti, pp. 157-158
[2] Ganesan: Ramana Periya Puranam, p. 255

do pastoral work in India, but was not allowed to give political speeches.

Ganesan writes: "The day His Holiness escaped to India, so did hundreds of fellow Tibetans. His Holiness came with many old Buddhist manuscripts, now preserved in the museum in Sarnath. Thus, thousands of priceless manuscripts were saved from the destructive hands of communist China. When the Dalai Lama entered India, Maurice planned it in such a manner, that Achyut Patwardhan would meet the Dalai Lama and give him the details. Yet, there is no mention of Maurice in any of the books related to either the Dalai Lama's escape or the smuggling in of Buddhist manuscripts from Tibet."[1]

Maurice wanted to settle the Tibetan refugees in various villages at an altitude of over 3,500 feet, as the climate there would be suitable for them. It was indeed a Herculean task to find villages for almost 80,000 refugees. No single state would take them all. Maurice worked out a plan to settle them in different parts of the country bordering Tibet with the help of the central government and went to Nehru. He waited in the Prime Minister's office until he agreed to speak to him. When he was finally listened to, he explained his plan. Nehru and the Indian government were worried that China might invade India next if they granted land to the Tibetan refugees. But he found an equal partner in Maurice, who refused to leave his office without an official letter that could be presented to the various Indian border states authorizing the use of land above 3,500 feet for Tibetan refugees.

Maurice left him with the letter and set off in search of land. He travelled to several states to find suitable locations for Tibetan refugee villages. In fact, he was able to establish three villages in Karnataka, where he was a trusted and widely

---

[1] ibid.

respected figure among the local officials. They are still thriving Tibetan communities today.

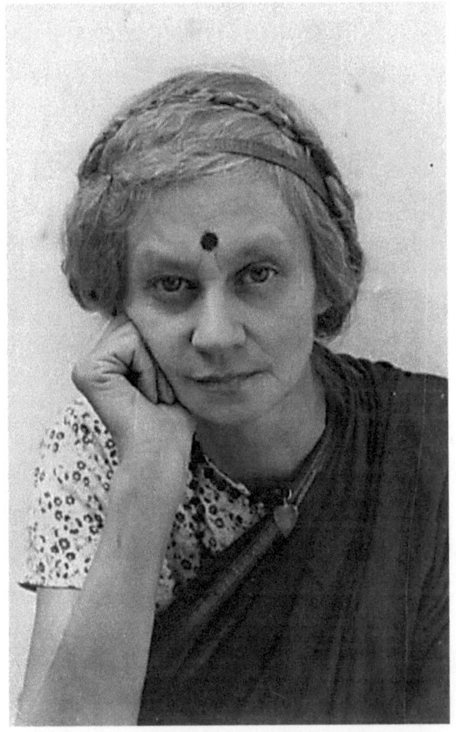

Uma Devi (Wanda Dynowska) (1888-1971)

Uma Devi also came to Sikkim and joined Maurice in organizing refugee camps and educational institutions for children with great zeal. In 1961, the Central Tibetan School Administration was established by the government to preserve the Tibetan language and culture. Uma Devi worked in Dharamsala, where the Dalai Lama had settled and established the exile government. The Dalai Lama later said that she helped the children there "like a second mother".

The refugee work kept Maurice busy from 1959 to 1965. When he was confronted with seemingly insurmountable difficulties with the authorities, he believed that ekagrata, determination, could achieve anything. The Indo-Chinese conflict broke out in 1962 when the Chinese occupied part of the Himalayas. Thousands of Tibetans fled to the vicinity of Nepal and Sikkim and were accommodated in Dharamsala. If the Tibetans are leading a peaceful life in India today, it is thanks to this Jewish mystic saint whose name is not mentioned anywhere.

Ganesan continues: "Discovering the capability of this man in bringing a semblance of order even in the most chaotic situations, Nehru requested Maurice to take over the khadi movement. It had initially been started by Gandhi, but was later in total disarray. This meant that Maurice had to go to Mumbai. Here, he stayed with an old friend of his, Miss Petit."[1]

Bary Gordon, who met Maurice in his later years, writes about Miss Petit: "Maurice was living on Nepean Sea Road at the home of Ms. Hirubhai Petit, a long-standing devotee of Sri Ramana Maharshi. Ms. Petit was a wonderful Parsi lady – a bit younger than Maurice – and almost deaf. She was generally seen only at mealtimes. Maurice and she had been constant companions for many years. [...]

Ms. Petit lived in the rooms in the front of the apartment and spent most of her time meditating. In her youth she had been a concert pianist, performing professionally in Europe, which was sometimes considered improper behavior for an Indian woman in those days.

Education was a rare option for women. I remember a Parsi woman, perhaps in her forties – a friend of both Maurice and Ms. Petit – who came by for lunch one day. She was one of the first female college graduates in India and was active in social work. She told me that Maurice had been instrumental in

---

[1] ibid. For Gandhi, hand-spun khadi was more than just a fabric. Weaving this fabric became a movement, a unifying force for the Indian people. The Khadi movement was based in Bombay (Mumbai).

helping her acquire higher education. He later provided her with great spiritual and emotional support when she was experiencing difficulty finding acceptance in the world of work, which was then completely dominated by men.

Maurice welcomed and fed everyone who came to his door – and many people came to his door. After sharply questioning me (as he did many of his guests – a skill Maurice was famous for), he offered me a trade. I could stay with him if I helped package and send to Poland the books he published.

I don't think Maurice needed to interrogate people, for he already knew the answers. It felt as if he held one's heart in the palms of his hands and could examine it in detail. From the sparkle in his eyes, though, he obviously enjoyed it. He saw everyone clearly and would allow no dishonesty. Quite a few deflated egos left his table better people."[1]

In Bombay, Maurice had met Nisargadatta Maharaj, who, like Ramana Maharshi, taught Advaita.[2]

"That was the beginning of an eighteen-month relationship during which I helped Maurice with many of his social projects, but mostly packing books for the Indo-Polish Library, helping him interview Nisargadatta Maharaj, and subsequently editing the manuscript to be published as I Am That. Although he didn't really need me to help with the book, for he was a brilliant writer in many languages, this work became one of the ways he taught me the importance of getting even the smallest detail right.

Together, we went to interview Nisargadatta Maharaj once each week, though I believe Maurice had started the interviews about a year before I met him. Maurice spoke Marathi (the local language) fluently, along with Hindi, Polish, Russian, French,

---

[1] www.geofengshui.com/gordon.htm
[2] for more details, see the following chapter

English, and several others. Maharaj was very fond of Maurice. Once, Maurice was injured in a collision with a motor scooter and couldn't leave the house for a few weeks.[1] We were surprised by a spontaneous visit from Maharaj, who had walked all the way with the help of one of his sons, concerned because Maurice had not shown up for his regular visit. Maharaj must have walked for more than an hour to reach Maurice's home.

Nisargadatta met visitors in a small room above his family's living quarters. He sat by the front window, with a bidi (country cigarette) in hand, and animatedly answered our questions, which were tape recorded by Maurice. [...]

Maharaj and Maurice were alike in many ways. They both were uncompromising concerning truth and had a similar intensity that could be mistaken for anger – but was more the fire of their enlightened compassion. In fact, all the teachers Maurice engaged were like this except perhaps Swami Ramdas. Although Maharaj is famous as a vedantin, I was amazed at the intensity of his puja (devotional worship). When the time came for puja, all conversation ceased; Maharaj grabbed his large cymbals and threw himself into worship-chanting at the top of his lungs – an example of true devotion. [...]

Though Maurice was already in his mid-seventies when I spent time with him, he was very active in various charities, most of which he had started and brought to fruition. Besides publishing spiritual books, he also started orphanages, homes to retrain prostitutes, and an organization to find dowries for them so they could marry. He was also in charge of India's Tibetan refugee program. He was closely associated with Chetana Books, a publisher and bookstore located in Bombay. (Chetana was the original publisher of I Am That, Maurice's collection of dialogues with Nisargadatta Maharaj.)

---

[1] This was probably the injury from which he ultimately died.

Maurice experimented with many things and was especially attracted to nature cures and special diets. I was being successfully treated by a homeopath for what I later realized was Agent Orange poisoning, contracted during my days as a Navy Diving Officer in Vietnam.[1] Maurice convinced me to switch to fasting, which started with three days of bananas, followed by three days of oranges, then three days of water only; then the reverse of this sequence. The homeopathy worked better. There were always strange concoctions on the table-dark liquids with unusual fragrances, etc. This must have gone on for years, because Pant also describes Maurice's fascination with food experiments. Gandhi also had this predilection. Maurice believed strongly in fasting and loved to recount the story of the Italian Count who lived during the Renaissance period. The Count was a great epicure who, because of his overindulgence, was grossly overweight. As a result of his weight problem, the Count became deathly ill. However, by simply cutting his food intake in half, the Count successfully restored his health."[2]

V. Ganesan visited Maurice in Bombay and wrote:

„I had earlier met him [Maurice] at the ashram in the 1960's during the rare visits that he made. Again, I met him when I went to Mumbai in the 70's to collect funds for the advertisements for Ramanasramam's journal, The Mountain Path. Maurice then told me, 'While your body is engaged in running the ashram[3], your heart should be totally settled in that pure awareness of truth. Never miss that, whatever you are doing.'

We used to have beautiful private conversations. […] On yet another occasion, he prodded me on, just to give me a push: 'See, Bhagavan is not the person. He is the teaching. As the

---

[1] Agent Orange was a toxic, plant-killing chemical (herbicide) used by the US military to clear foliage during the Vietnam conflict. It led to various diseases.
[2] www.geofengshui.com/gordon.htm
[3] V. Ganesan was involved in running the ashram at the time.

teaching, he is fully available to you. In addition to whatever work you are doing, plunge within and taste awareness inwardly. That awareness is our Bhagavan.'

Maurice used to take me for long walks in Mumbai. He would tell me, 'I will not provide you with a car; I will not even take you by bus; you have to walk wherever you go, along with me. Are you prepared?' With hands folded in a namaste, I would answer, 'Would I hesitate to be in the proximity the truth of reality?'

Maurice was a spiritual giant, but physically he was less than five feet tall. Surely no one would hesitate to walk next to him!"[1]

---

[1] Ganesan: Ramana Periya Puranam, pp. 255-256

In 1976, Maurice was hit by a motorcycle and broke his hip. He was too weak to be operated on and was confined to bed from then on.

V. Ganesan could not be present when Maurice died. He reports:

„I was unable to be with Maurice Frydman in his last days. But I was happy to understand from a devotee of Bhagavan who was also Nisargadatta Maharaj's devotee, that Bhagavan himself looked after him. The devotee told me about a nurse in Mumbai who normally charged a huge fee for her services. This nurse had a dream, in which a sadhu wearing only a loin cloth told her very clearly, 'My devotee is suffering. Go and attend on him.' The sadhu also gave her precise directions to reach Maurice's residence. The nurse went to the place described in the dream the next day and found Maurice Frydman in bed. Miss Petit was older than Maurice and she too was helpless and unattended. The nurse immediately offered her services. Maurice's austere attitude would not allow him to accept her services and so he refused. Disappointed, the nurse was leaving the room when she saw a picture of Ramana Maharshi there. She turned to Maurice and exclaimed, 'This is the sadhu who appeared in my dream.' Maurice, visibly moved, said, 'So, my master has come to look after me.' The nurse served him till the end."

On March 9, 1976, Maurice died of multiple organ failure.

Ganesan reports further:

"Once, I went to Nisargadatta Maharaj's house because he had asked me to stay with him. I stayed there for eight days. In the morning, from eight to ten, he would ask me to be seated while he did pooja. There were photographs of saints such as Ramakrishna Paramahamsa, the Buddha, Jesus Christ, Ramana Maharshi, and yes, even Maurice Frydman, in his room. Maharaj would apply sandal, vermillion powder and perfume to the photographs and garland them. As he was doing this ritual one day, I was asking myself, 'Why is he doing this?' He turned to me and said in a compassionate tone, 'Maurice Frydman was a jnani. He was a saint, a sage.'"[1]

---

[1] ibid., pp. 256-257

Maurice Frydman and Ramana Maharshi

Maurice Frydman with suit

As already mentioned, Maurice Frydman came across Paul Brunton's book "A Search in Secret India" in 1935. In it, Brunton recounts his encounter with Ramana Maharshi, the great sage from Arunachala in Tiruvannamalai, South India. This book, which was published in 1934, led many Westerners to the Maharshi, including Maurice.

Maurice came to India in 1935. He never returned to his homeland as his family perished in the Second World War. As already seen, he was entrusted with the construction of a large factory for the manufacture of electrical appliances in Bangalore.

As a boy of 16, Ramana Maharshi had unexpectedly experienced the immortal self during a death experience. This experience was constant and never left him. Soon afterwards he left home and settled on the holy hill of Arunachala. In the 1920s, Ramanashram was built at the foot of the hill, where he could be found until his death. He attracted people from near and far and taught them Atma Vichara, self-enquiry with the question: "Who am I?"[1]

Ramana Maharshi

People called Ramana the Maharshi (great sage) and addressed him reverently as Bhagavan, which means Lord or God.

---

[1] For more information on Ramana Maharshi see Ebert: Ramana Maharshi: His life

An unknown author reports in "The Mountain Path" about Maurice's first encounter with the Maharshi in September 1935:

"One morning in September, one Maurice Frydman, a consulting and electrical engineer announced himself before Sri Bhagavan. He entered the Hall, hat in hand but with shoes on. The Maharshi ordered a stool for him on which he seated himself cross-legged for a short time and then he withdrew.

After a wash and light refreshments he came back without shoes and squatted on the floor. He stayed three days and was quite social and genial and friendly to everyone who responded similarly towards him. He tried to learn our ways and adapt himself to them. His clumsiness often evoked the good-humoured laughter of the Maharshi who always put him right as a father would a child.

He tried to learn from Maharshi something about Realisation, raised doubts and had them cleared. Once he asked why there should be illusion if the individual soul is identical with the supreme. Bhagavan gave him the usual answer (the answer is not given in the text) and then began to chew betel leaves. In the meantime, Mr. Frydman was ruminating and with dramatic gestures wanted to know why the ego should not be cut down at one stroke and destroyed so as to gain Supreme Bliss. The Maharshi stopped chewing his betel leaves long enough to smile, and then broke out into laughter and asked the questioner to hold out his ego so that the Maharshi could strike it down. Everyone in the Hall laughed including Mr. Frydman, and at the conclusion of the laughter. Mr. Frydman addressed the Maharshi and said, 'Yes, now I understand.'"[1]

Maurice Frydman reports the following about his encounter with Ramana Maharshi:

---

[1] The Mountain Path 1981, April, p. 69

"Just six months after I came to India, I was left alone and had no friends. The person whom I loved died and I had nothing to attract me in life. Quite accidentally, just for fun, I dropped in at Tiruvannamalai. I went direct to the swami but I was ordered out by his disciples as I had not taken off my shoes.

After bathing and other preparations, I went again to the hall and remained there with the Maharshi for two hours. Then I understood that I had met someone, the likes of whom I had never met before. I did not then know what was meant by words like Maharshi and Bhagavan. I had no preconceived ideas and yet I felt that there was something extraordinary in that man.

I was told about his teachings but they were far too high for me. I did not understand what they meant but I felt a strong and lasting affection for him. I was alone in India and I attached myself to him just as a homeless dog would to his master.

Afterwards, whenever I felt worried, I used to go to Arunachala, and sit in his presence. In the early days I would be asking questions, but later when I began to visit him more and more, the discussion with him grew less and less.

Then I began to visit him almost every month. I knew no sadhana or dhyana. I would simply sit in his presence. To my questions, Sri Maharshi would say: 'Find out who you are.' I could not make out anything but all the same I felt happy. Slowly some change came in me. Just as the egg grows and hatches only with the aid of the warmth of the mother I was also getting into shape slowly and steadily in his presence. My mind became more quiet than before. Previously it was unhappy and never satisfied. Now a kind of security and peace began to be felt spontaneously.

I felt that Sri Maharshi was coming nearer and nearer as time passed. Afterwards I used to think of him whenever I felt unhappy. He used to appear before me and ask if I have not committed any sin. If I had erred or sinned, he used to hide himself for a time but later on appear and reply. His affection was always there and as fire melts ice so his affection made my worries melt."[1]

Maurice worked day and night in the factory in Bangalore and became very successful within a short time. On weekends, he went to Ramanashram.

The people in the Ashram said about his frequent weekly visits: "Maurice, why don't you come once a month or maybe once every two months? You have to spend so much to come here." Maurice replied, "What can I do? My battery can take only so much. Within a week it dries up. I have to come here every week to be in Bhagavan's presence and get it recharged!"[2]

Maurice read about Vedanta and the Hindu scriptures and discussed them with others. He also read that one had to take sannyas if one wanted final liberation. Finally, he approached Ramana and asked, "Bhagavan, this is what the Hindu scriptures say. Will you please give me sannyas?"

Ramana remained silent, but Maurice did not give up easily.

One day he approached Ramana on the hill and said, "Bhagavan, give me sannyas. I want to renounce the world and strive towards enlightenment."

Ramana replied in a very compassionate tone, "Sannyas is taken from within, not from without."

He looked at Maurice like a mother and explained, "You are already a sannyasin. Why do you want to take up ochre robes?"

---

[1] Reminiscences by Maurice Frydman, in: The Silent Power, Selections from The Mountain Path and the Call Divine, 2002 https://archive.arunachala.org/docs/silent-p#rem.9
[2] Ganesan: Ramana Periya Purana, p. 252

Maurice did not give up. He kept asking Ramana for sannyas, and Ramana always answered, "There is no need for sann-yas."[1]

So what did Maurice do with his brilliant, inventive mind? He went to Swami Ramdas, a realized soul in the Anandashram.

Swami Ramdas with his disciple Krishnabai

Swami Ramdas had once been a family man and had owned his own company that dyed saris. Dissatisfied with life, he turned to religious practice and constantly repeated the mantra "Om Ram Jai Ram Jai Jai Ram" (Om, victory to Rama). He left his

---

[1] ibid.

family, wandered all over India as a mendicant monk and finally founded the Anandashram in Kanhangad, Kerala.

Somehow Maurice convinced Swami Ramdas to give him sannyas. Swami Ramdas gave him the outer sannyas that he so desperately wanted. He was given the name Swami Bharatananda, which means something like "one who likes to stay in India".

Maurice stayed at Andashram for a few months. Once Swami Ramdas said to him, "Maurice, Swami Bharatananda, this is your last birth." Being a great sage, he could understand the greatness of Maurice.

When Maurice returned to Ramanashram, he met Ramana just as he was coming down the hill from his walk. Maurice was now standing in front of him in the ochre-coloured robes of a Hindu monk. He was quite worried because he wanted his master to approve of what he had done. When Ramana saw him, he began to laugh, turned to his attendant who was accompanying him and said, "Hey, he looks like a buffoon in a circus."

Maurice understood. All his life, he had been a true sannyasin from the inside out. Consequently, his attachment to wearing ochre robes lasted only a few more years and he gradually gave it up.

Even when he was working in the factory, Maurice led a very strict life. He refused to accept his monthly salary of three thousand rupees – an incredibly high sum for the time. He refused the amount with the words: "I do not want it. Give it to the workers' fund."[1]

At night, he slept on the veranda of a store. While all the other workers streamed into the dining hall to eat the lunch they had

---

[1] The company retained his salary to pay him later. When Maurice left the company, they paid him the entire outstanding amount and he distributed this large sum to the neediest of his workers.

brought from home, Maurice stood at the entrance in his ochre-coloured robe with his begging bowl in his hand. This was in the spirit of a true sannyasin. The workers, who loved him very much, first put something in the begging bowl before they went into the dining hall to eat. And not only that: Maurice sewed his own clothes. He only wore khadi pyjamas and kurtas made from the yarn he had spun himself on the charkha, the traditional Indian spinning wheel. Even his footwear was stitched by himself. He led a remarkably simple life, but he was happy and content. He did not boast about his way of life, nor did he abandon it.

As already mentioned, he was very successful professionally. The transformers manufactured in the factory since 1936 were used to implement the first rural electrification program in the Indian princely state of Mysore.

Maurice's relationship with Ramana remained close. He asked him many questions about the practical aspects of sadhana. Ramana answered them patiently. Maurice recorded these conversations and then showed them to Ramana to have them corrected. He also collected other conversations. This collection was published in 1939 as Maharshi's Gospel on the occasion of Ramana's sixtieth birthday. His name was not even mentioned in the first edition. This was only made up for in the later edition. Some of Maurice's conversations have also been handed down in the extensive "Talks with Sri Ramana Maharshi".

Maurice always behaved very bluntly and directly. Once when Ramana was ill, he gave the ashram administrator 1,000 rupees to buy fruit for him. Since the ashram manager knew that Ramana would only eat if everyone else received the same, he spent the money on something else. A few months later, Maurice complained to Ramana that his money had not been used properly. Ramana replied angrily, "When you give something you should regard the matter as closed. How dare you use this gift to further your ego?"[1]

Godman writes:

"This was Maurice being his typical bulldozery self. He walked in to Ramana and thought, this man is not eating properly. I will put him on a better diet. So he went off, bought a couple of oranges, hand squeezed them, brought them in, put them on a tray and said, 'You need more vitamins. Drink this.' And Bhagavan of course never consumed anything that he couldn't share equally with everybody in the hall. So he waved his hand around saying, 'What about these 200 people here?', as a way of saying, 'No, thank you.'

But to Maurice, that was just a challenge. He went to town and bought every single orange he could find and hand squeezed 200 glasses of orange juice. He had them all paraded in on a big tray and gave everybody, the 200 people, a glass each; and then he gave Bhagavan his glass and said, 'Now you can't refuse. Everybody else has had a glass first.' And Bhagavan said, 'Ok, you have made your point. I will take it. But don't do this again. It is not necessary.'

That's just the way he was. He was just a man who saw things, thought they needed to be changed, and took action and got them done."[2]

Maurice also wrote a series of moving poems. Ramana read them with great interest. In one of them he says:

"So long I have been on this stage to please thee.
My eyes are blinded by the light of thy play.
My ears are deafened by the rolling thunder of thy laughter.

---

[1] Face to Face, p. 204
[2] https://www.wisdom2be.com/essays-insights-wisdomwritings-spirituality/david-godman-interview-buddha-and-the-gas-pump-excerpt-on-maurice-frydman

My heart is turned to ashes by the flame of real sorrow.
My lord, to please thee I have made a fool of myself.
And now I am unable to stop the agony of the play.
My lord, drag me down from this stage.
Master, I have forgotten the way in and the way out."[1]

"Bhagavan was happy to read through the verses. He said that this was exactly what had been written by Appayya Dikshitar, a sage who lived several centuries ago. His verses in Sanskrit were written on palm leaves and many people were not aware of them. Bhagavan said that Appaya Dikshitar's verses describe the situation of the court dancer performing in the presence of the king. She cannot stop dancing unless it pleases the king to tell her to stop. The dancer's limbs may ache but she cannot stop of her own accord. She cries, 'Oh lord, I am weary of the many births and deaths that I have endured. One glance from you, oh lord, is sufficient to put an end to this dance of birth and death and grant me release.'

Bhagavan paused before saying, 'Maurice Frydman belongs here. Somehow, he was born abroad but he has come here again. Otherwise, how is it possible for him to compose verses similar to Appayya Dikshitar?'"[2]

But Maurice still had to appear on the world stage because he was a karma yogi who still had many good deeds to do. So he resigned himself to the course of events. He worked in the factory for three years and regularly visited the ashram. Then he turned to the Aundh experiment. Wherever he was, he remained in correspondence with Ramana.

In one of his letters to Ramana, he wrote: "The Maharshi is with me not only when I think of him, but also when I am not thinking of him. Otherwise, how do I live?"[3]

---

[1] Ganesan: Ramana Periya Puranam, pp. 253-254
[2] ibid.
[3] ibid.

The state of Aundh was a small Maratha princely state which belonged to the Deccan States Agency Division of the Bombay Presidency and had already been founded in 1699. The capital was Aundh. At that time, there were 675 such princely states, large and small, in British India. The rulers of these states, who were called Rajas, Maharajas, Nawabs etc. depending on the size of their estates, had considerable freedom to rule their territories as they saw fit. Bhawanrao Pant was an enlightened ruler who tried to preserve the cultural and spiritual heritage of his small state. His princely state was only 1300 square kilometres in size. It was also a poor state that had been ravaged by a plague epidemic in 1911 and suffered from frequent famines. It consisted of 75 tiny, impoverished villages.

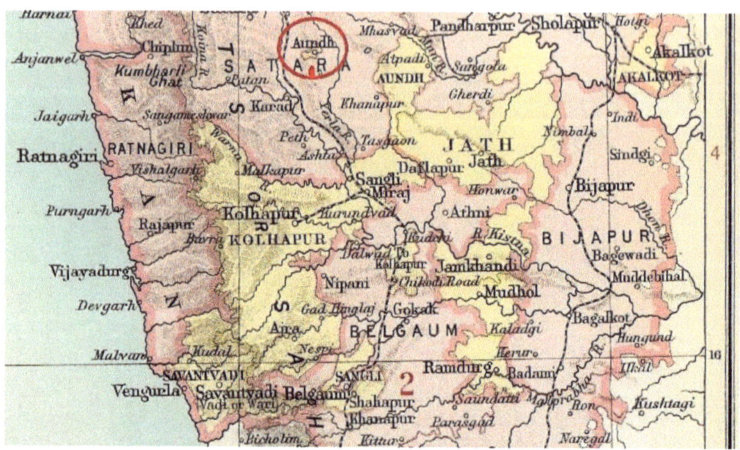

The capital Aundh in the centre above,
Imperial Gazetteer of India 1909

The "Aundh experiment", as it was called, i.e. the democratization of the small princely state, was not well received by the other princely states, who feared the loss of their power, but it was well received by the population.

As we have seen, Raja Bhawanrao sent his eldest son Apa Pant to study in England. Apa Pant studied in Oxford and London and returned after 4 years to later work as a lawyer. The Raja sent him to the great princely state of Mysore in the south to train him in general administration as Mysore's excellent administration was well known. As part of the training, he was asked to visit several factories there. Maurice's electrical factory was also on this list.

Subsequently, Maurice started working with Apa Pant on the Aundh experiment. He heard about Mahatma Gandhi's great interest in bringing decentralized democracy to the villages. So he set out to meet Gandhi and learn more about the process. Gandhi immediately took a liking to Maurice. He addressed him only by his monk's name, Bharatananda, and everyone in his Sevagram Ashram addressed him in the same way.

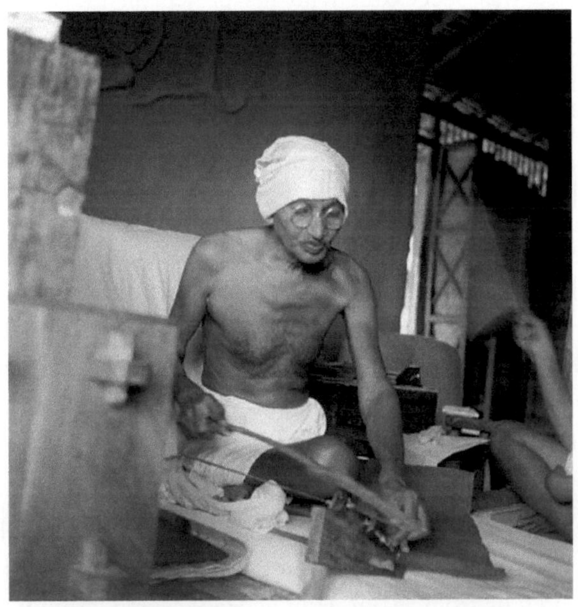
Gandhi spins with the Dhanush Takli, 1940

Gandhi realized that Maurice was not only a hard worker but also an inventor who used the Indian charkha (spinning wheel) himself. He asked him: "Why don't you invent something with which we can make yarn faster?" Maurice invented several spinning wheels, including one called Dhanush Takli. The extraordinary thing about the new invention was that three times as much yarn could be produced with the same amount of work as the traditional charkha. Gandhi was naturally delighted.

Maurice's association with Gandhi continued until the latter was assassinated in 1948.

After some time, Maurice drafted a new constitution for Aundh, which transferred political power from the Raja to the people – the first princely state to introduce a republic within the Indian Union.

Maurice was successful with his project in the villages. He loved the poor, uneducated villagers and was very compassionate towards them. They addressed him respectfully as "Swami".

Ramana Maharshi died on April 14, 1950. Maurice wrote in an article:

"The burning regret which many, probably, share with me, is that full advantage was not taken of those happy and precious days when He was with us physically also – eating, talking, laughing, welcoming all, open to all. Reality was there – in abundance and for the taking, but we enclosed ourselves in timidity, in false humility, in self-deprecation and false excuses. We took a cupful when the ocean was at our feet.

Now He is still with us, but no longer so easily accessible. To find Him again we must overcome the very obstacles which prevented us from seeing Him as He was and going with Him where He wanted to take us. It was tamas and rajas – fear and desire that stood in the way – the desire for the pleasure of the past and fear of austere responsibility of a higher state of being. It was the same old story – the threshold of maturity of mind and heart which most of us refuse to cross. 'Ripeness is all' He used to say – and now ripeness is the condition of finding Him again.

We ripen when we refuse to drift, when striving ceaselessly becomes a way of life, when dispassion born of insight becomes spontaneous. When the search Who Am I? becomes the only thing that matters, when we become a mere torch and the flame all-important, it will mean that we are ripening fast. We cannot accelerate that ripening – but we can remove the obstacles of fear and greed, indolence and fancy, prejudice and pride. He is there and waiting – timelessly. It is we who keep Him waiting."[1]

[1] Bharatananda: Readiness, in: The Mountain Path, 1976, April, p. 66

Maurice Frydman and
Nisargadatta Maharaj

Nisargadatta, 1973

Nisargadatta Maharaj (1897-1981) was a sage in the advaitic tradition, similar to Ramana Maharshi. He was modest, without much education, spoke only Marathi and earned his living by selling beedis, local cigarettes in which the tobacco is stuffed into a dried leaf and tied together with a string. He lived in a loft-like tenement in a crowded part of Bombay, was a disciple of Siddharameshwar Maharaj, a self-realized master, and was a family man. Especially those who were attracted to the advaitic path and self-inquiry in the style of Ramana flocked to him.

Maurice was living with Hilla Petit near Nisargadatta's home in Bombay. He met him on the street at one of his speeches in 1965 and became his disciple.

Nisargadatta second from left, Maurice Frydman third from right
with white hair and glasses

V. Ganesan visited Maurice in Bombay. He reports what Maurice had told him about his first encounter with Nisargadatta:

„On one of these walks, Maurice said, 'Ganesan, today I am going to take you to the place where I met a simple man selling beedis.'

As we were walking towards the place, Maurice narrated,

'I saw a group of people smoking beedis; they were relating their woes of life. This simple man answered them exactly in the manner of Ramana Maharshi. Had Ramana Maharshi spoken in Marathi, it would have been the same! I stopped in my tracks and listened intently. It was astounding to see an ordinary man selling beedis talking so spontaneously! I started going to the place every day and noting down what he says. I would then go home and translate all the questions and answers into English.'

However, Maurice was ridden with guilt because he had not sought the permission of this person. He informed the man what he had been doing and read out all his writings, translating them into Marathi. The man was delighted and told Maurice, 'Go on recording, go ahead!'

This was later published as I am That – a publication that shook the entire spiritual world. This man was none other than Nisargadatta Maharaj.

Later on, after I had met Maharaj, I told Maurice, 'Whatever you say is absolutely true. I can feel Bhagavan's presence in his presence. The teaching of Bhagavan comes from him spontaneously.'

Maurice always used to encourage me, 'Come on and narrate to me the dialogue that you had with Maharaj.' He would add, 'Being a spiritual seeker, associating with sages and saints will deepen your understanding; it will help you go deeper and experience it. Reading improves only intellectual understanding. This experience oriented understanding will happen, whether you have understood it or not, only in the presence of realized masters.' Saying this, he encouraged me to go to Maharaj."[1]

Nisargadatta's conversations with the visitors were recorded on tape. Maurice, who spoke Marathi, translated them into English. When he visited him, he often acted as a translator for visitors who did not understand Marathi. This is how the extensive book "I Am That" came into being. There is also a Marathi version of it.

This book has become a classic in this field. It became so popular in the West that many seekers flocked to Nisargadatta's small lane in Bombay. Hundreds of foreigners crowded into his home, and Maharaj himself commented: "I used to have a quiet life, but I am That has turned my house into a railway station platform."[2]

---

[1] Ganesan: Ramana Periya Puranam, p. 256
[2] Srinivasan: Maurice Frydman, p. [34]

Publishing the book proved difficult at first, as many well-known publishers did not want to bring it out. It was finally published in 1973 by the small publishing house Chetana Books with great success.

Much later David Godman asked Nisargadatta: "In all the years you have been teaching, how many people have actually understood what you were saying and experienced it?" And he said, "One. Maurice Frydman."[1] He regarded Maurice as a fully realized Jnani.

Maurice wrote about Nisargadatta:

"In the humble abode of Sri Nisargadatta Maharaj, but for the electric lights and the noises of the street traffic, one would not know in which period of human history one dwells. There is an atmosphere of timelessness about his tiny room; the subjects discussed are timeless; the way they are expounded and examined is also timeless; the centuries, millennia and yugas fall off and one deals with matters immensely ancient and eternally new.

The discussions held and teachings given would have been the same ten thousand years ago and will be the same ten thousand years hence. There will always be conscious beings wondering about the fact of their being conscious and inquiring into its cause and aim. Whence am I? Who am I? Whither am I? Such questions have no beginning and no end. And it is crucial to know the answers, for without a full understanding of oneself, both in time and in timelessness, life is but a dream, imposed on us by powers we do not know, for purposes we cannot grasp.

Maharaj is not a learned man. There is no erudition behind his homely Marathi; authorities he does not quote, scriptures are rarely mentioned; the astonishingly rich spiritual heritage of

---

[1] https://www.wisdom2be.com/essays-insights-wisdomwritings-spirituality/david-godman-interview-buddha-and-the-gas-pump-excerpt-on-maurice-frydman

India is implicit in him rather than explicit. No rich Ashram was ever built round him and most of his followers are humble working people cherishing the opportunity of spending an hour with him.

Simplicity and humility are the keynotes of his life and teachings; physically and inwardly he never takes the higher seat; the essence of being on which he talks, he sees in others as clearly as he sees it in himself. He admits that while he is aware of it, others are not yet, but this difference is temporary and of little importance, except to the mind and its ever-changing content. When asked about his Yoga, he says he has none to offer, no system to propound, no theology, cosmogony, psychology or philosophy. He knows the real nature – his own and his listeners' – and he points it out. The listener cannot see it because he cannot see the obvious, simply and directly. All he knows, he knows with his mind, stimulated by the senses. That the mind is a sense in itself, he does not even suspect.

The Nisarga Yoga[1], the 'natural' Yoga of Maharaj, is disconcertingly simple – the mind, which is all-becoming, must recognize and penetrate its own being, not as being this or that, here or there, then or now, but just timeless being.

This timeless being is the source of both life and consciousness. In terms of time, space and causation it is all-powerful, being the cause less cause; all-pervading, eternal, in the sense of being beginningless, endless and ever-present. Uncaused, it is free; all-pervading, it knows; undivided, it is happy. It lives, it loves, and it has endless fun, shaping and reshaping the universe. Every man has it, every man is it, but not all know themselves as they are, and therefore identify themselves with the name and shape of their bodies and the contents of their consciousness.

---

[1] nisarga: natural state, innate disposition

To rectify this misunderstanding of one's reality, the only way is to take full cognizance of the ways of one's mind and to turn it into an instrument of self-discovery. The mind was originally a tool in the struggle for biological survival. It had to learn the laws and ways of nature in order to conquer it. That it did, and is doing, for mind and nature working hand-in-hand can raise life to a higher level. But, in the process the mind acquired the art of symbolic thinking and communication, the art and skill of language. Words became important. Ideas and abstractions acquired an appearance of reality, the conceptual replaced the real, with the result that man now lives in a verbal world, crowded and dominated by words.

Obviously, for dealing with things and people words are exceedingly useful. But they make us live in a world totally symbolic and unreal. To break out from this prison of the verbal mind into reality, one must be able to shift one's focus from the word to what it refers to.

The most commonly used word and most pregnant with feelings, and ideas is the word 'I'. Mind tends to include in it anything and everything, the body as well as the Absolute. In practice it stands as a pointer to an experience, which is direct, immediate and immensely significant. To be, and to know that one is, is most important. And to be of interest, a thing must be related to one's conscious existence, which is the focal point of every desire and fear. For, the ultimate aim of every desire is to enhance and intensify this sense of existence, while all fear is, in its essence, the fear of self-extinction.

To delve into the sense of 'I' – so real and vital – in order to reach its source is the core of the Nisarga Yoga. Not being continuous, the sense of 'I' must have a source from which it flows and to which it returns. This timeless source of conscious being is what Maharaj calls the self-nature, self-being, swarupa.

As to methods of realizing one's supreme identity with the self-being, Maharaj is peculiarly noncommittal. He says that each has his own way to reality. But, for all the gateway to reality, by whatever road one arrives to it, is the sense of 'I am'. It is through grasping the full import of the 'I am', and going beyond it to its source, that one can realize the ultimate, supreme state. The difference between the beginning and the end lies only in the mind. When the mind is dark or turbulent, the source is not perceived. When it is clear and luminous, it becomes a faithful reflection of the source. The source is always the same – beyond darkness and light, beyond life and death, beyond the conscious and the unconscious.

Maharaj, unknown, Maurice Frydman in the 1970s

This dwelling on the sense 'I am' is the simple, easy and natural Yoga, the Nisarga Yoga. There is no secrecy in it and no dependence; no preparation or initiation is required. Whoever is puzzled by his very existence as a conscious being and earnestly wants to find his own source, can grasp the ever-present sense of 'I am' and dwell on it assiduously and patiently, till the clouds obscuring the mind dissolve and the heart of being is seen in all its glory.

The Nisarga Yoga, when persevered in and brought to its fruition, results in one becoming conscious and active in what one always was unconsciously and passively. There is no difference in kind – only in manner – the difference between a lump of gold and a glorious ornament shaped out of it. Life goes on, but it is spontaneous and free, meaningful and happy.

Maharaj most lucidly describes this natural, spontaneous state, but as the man born blind cannot visualize light and colors, so is the unenlightened mind unable to give meaning to such descriptions. Expressions like dispassionate happiness, affectionate detachment, timelessness and causelessness of things and being – they all sound strange and cause no response. Intuitively we feel they have deep meaning, and they even create in us a strange longing for the ineffable, a forerunner of things to come, but that is all. As Maharaj puts it; words are pointers, they show the direction but they will not come along with us. Truth is the fruit of earnest action, words merely point the way."[1]

---

[1] Nisargadatta: I Am That, Appendix I: Nisarga Yoga, pp. 512-515

Bibliography

Apa Pant: A Moment in Time, London, 1974

Apa Pant: An Unusual Raja: Mahatma Gandhi and the Aundh experiment, Hyderabad, 1989

Apa Pant: Maurice Frydman, in: The Mountain Path, Aradhana Issue 1991, pp. 31-36 und Jayanti Issue 1991, pp. 125-128

Apa Pant in Wikipedia:
https://en.wikipedia.org/wiki/Apa_Pant

Aundh-Experiment in Wikipedia:
https://en.wikipedia.org/wiki/Aundh_Experiment

V. Ganesan: Ramana Periya Purana (Inner Journey of 75 Old Devotees, pp. 251-258
free download: https://www.aham.com/RamanaPeriyaPuranam/RamanaPeriyaPuranam.pdf

David Godman in an interview about Maurice Frydman:
https://www.wisdom2be.com/essays-insights-wisdomwritings-spirituality/david-godman-interview-buddha-and-the-gas-pump-excerpt-on-maurice-frydman

Ebert, Gabriele: Ramana Maharshi: His Life, Norderstedt, 2015

Face to Face with Sri Ramana: Enchanting and Uplifting Reminiscences of 202 persons, complied and ed. by Laxmi Narain, Hyderabad, 2009

F.M. [Frydman, Maurice]: How I understand Krishnamurti, Chapter 18, in: The Mind of J. Krishnamurti, ed. By Luis S.R. Vas, Bombay, (n.d.), pp. 157-158

Frydman, Maurice: Man and Machine, in: Gandhi: His Life and Work, Bombay, 1944, pp. 140-150

Gordon, Barry: Maurice Frydman:
www.geofengshui.com/gordon.htm

Jiddu, Krishnamurti: Exploration into Insight, Chapter 9: The Chattering Mind: a discussion with Maurice Frydman and others in Bombay on 22 January 1973
https://jkrishnamurti.org/content/chapter-9-chattering-mind-discussion-bombay-22-january-1973

Maharshi's Gospel: books 1 & 2: The teachings of Ramana Maharshi, Tiruvannamalai, 2002

Nisargadatta Maharaj: I am That, 16th printing, Mumbai, 2009

N.K. Srinivasan: Maurice Frydman – Jnani and a Karma Yogi: A Biography: https://de.scribd.com/document/97304328/Maurice-Frydman-a-Jnani-and-a-Karma-Yogi

Talks with Sri Ramana Maharshi, Tiruvannamalai, 2010

(Retrieval date online documents, 04.01.2025)